How to Read the Bible

A Tool to Enhance Your Reading Experience

Janice Hilton

Directed Copy
Yucaipa, California

ISBN-10: 0692884491
ISBN-13: 978-0692884492

Printed in the United States of America

Directed Copy

BestBibleToBuy.com

Table of Contents

Chapters   **Page**

1. Why read this book?   1

2. Where do you begin?   3

3. What will you read in the Bible?   5

4. What's your first step?   11

5. If you're a beginner   15

6. If you have some Bible experience   19

7. If you're on an academic quest   29

8. One final note   33

9. Bible reading schedules   35

Appendices

Appendix A – New Testament Reading Schedule   37

Appendix B – Daily Bible Reading Schedule 1   39

Appendix C – Daily Bible Reading Schedule 2   49

Appendix D – Scripture Used in this Book   55

1

Why read this book?

Does it seem strange that I think you should read a book about how to read a book? If the Bible were an ordinary book, perhaps it would be strange. But the Bible is unlike any other book you can buy or read.

Even though it is the Holy Book for the world's largest religion, it has some unusual characteristics that make it a little challenging to read through.

- It contains sixty-six separate books
- Some of these books are very long
- Some of these books contain mystical symbolic writing
- You'll find lists and lists of names that are hard to pronounce
- It outlines laws that seem obscure and irrelevant
- Some of the writing is rooted in cultures that are long dead, making them hard to understand and apply

And yet, millions of people buy it, read it and love it. It outsells every other book that has ever been published.

This little book about how to read the Bible was written to help you understand how the Bible is put together, making it easier to read. It will give you practical tips on how to proceed.

It is intended for those who are new to the Bible, for those who know the Bible but have never read through it and for those who have a scholarly or historic interest in its contents. It will give you insight into the Bible's structure and provide information about options for how to read it all the way through, a feat that many people find daunting.

This book is not written to try to convince you that the Bible is true or is from God. I believe that it is, but that's not the purpose of this book. There are many books available that you can read for that information.

And there are many books you can read to dig deep into particular passages or themes of the Bible. This book will not provide that kind of inspiration. The focus of this book is very narrow and meant to be a tool to help you read through the Bible for the first time, or even the first few times.

So, let's get started.

2

Where do you begin?

The first thing you want to determine when you are ready to read the Bible through for the first time is this: What do you hope to gain from the experience? Knowing this will help determine the best approach for you to take.

You may be a new Christian or on a spiritual journey, looking for answers to some of the deep questions about your life. In either case, you will probably be looking for some foundational information about who Jesus is, what He said, what He did and what implications His teachings and His actions might have on your life. If so, the best place to begin is the New Testament portion of the Bible. Located at the end of the Bible, it focuses on the life and ministry of Jesus and the foundation of the Church.

Or perhaps you've been a Christian for a while, maybe even for years. You've had the chance to hear sermons, participate in a Bible study group or some Bible classes. You may have read some portions of the Bible several times, and perhaps you have some favorite passages or a favorite book. You may have even tried, unsuccessfully, to read the Bible all the way through or decided that this should be your next step. It can be a challenging task. You need a system to make the task manageable. The most balanced approach for you is to read the Old and New Testaments simultaneously.

If your interest is more scholastic in nature you could just begin at the first page of the Bible and read through to the end, like any other book. But this can be quite intimidating even for a disciplined student. Some of the books are too long to read in a single setting and must be read in portions. Navigating the different types of literature and discerning the different cultures represented by the authors and their initial audience is made easier with some background information. And understanding the relationships between the different books and their authors will make for a richer, more memorable experience. You will want to give careful consideration to which version and format of the Bible you choose.

Each of these three options will be discussed in detail. If you find yourself described above, you may want to go directly to the chapter that will help you the most. Or you may want to read through all the options to see which fits. But before we move to specifics there are some things you should know about the Bible that will make your reading experience more profitable.

3

What will you read in the Bible?

It is helpful when reading the Bible to know how it is constructed. There are sixty-six books written by forty different authors. Each book is divided into numbered chapters and each chapter has numbered verses. So, when you see a verse reference like John 3:16 it is referring to the book of John, chapter 3, verse 16.

The Bible is divided into two main parts, the Old Testament and the New Testament. The Old Testament is about God's relationship with mankind before Jesus was born, and in particular His relationship with the nation of Israel.

The New Testament is about Jesus and about how His coming established a way for mankind to have a new type of relationship with God. And in the same way that a library is organized by type of literature, the Bible is organized by type of literature.

The Old Testament

There are three types of literature in the Old Testament in this order: history, poetry and prophecy books. This means that you will not always be reading things in chronological order.

For instance, the story of Moses and the exodus from Egypt is found in the second book of the Bible, the book of Exodus, which is in the history section. The stories of King David of Israel are found later in the history books, as they happened much later. But in the poetry section, in the book of Psalms, a big collection of poems (150 in all), the early poems are written by King David, but Psalm 90 was written by Moses.

It's important when you are reading the Bible to note which kind of literature you are reading. In your everyday reading for instance, you read the account of an event from a newspaper or from the internet differently than you read song lyrics. You accept that a song or a poem will use words that may be figurative, rather than literal. But you expect a news report to be factual and to the point.

And when you read factual accounts, it helps to know if the account was written by an eye witness or not. It helps to know that the book or article was written a few days ago or a hundred years ago. Both are valuable, but you look for different insights from each. You can expect the same interactions with the different types of literature in the Bible. Knowing which kind of literature you are reading will help you understand it.

The history books are in chronological order from Genesis through Esther. They are primarily about the history of the nation of Israel. The book of Genesis tells of Adam and Eve, Cain and Abel, Noah and the flood, and the tower of Babel. Then we meet Abraham, whose family becomes the nation of Israel. You may recognize some of the stories from the other history books, such as Moses and the Ten Commandments, the battle of Jericho, Samson and Delilah, and David and Goliath.

Five poetry books come next: Job, Psalms, Proverbs, Ecclesiastes and the Song of Solomon. You may think of poems as being rhymes, but this poetry is much more. Only Psalms and the Song of Solomon are classic poetry.

The book of Psalms includes the well know Psalm 23 which starts "The Lord is my shepherd, I shall not want" and includes many other beautiful poems and songs. Proverbs, as the name indicates, is a collection of proverbs; Ecclesiastes is a philosophical treatise on life and its meaning. The Song of Solomon is an extended love poem. And you have probably heard references to Job whose life was filled with trouble. It begins as a dialogue between Job and his friends and then takes an amazing twist near the end.

And finally there are the books of prophecy. They span from Isaiah to Malachi and are generally named for the prophet who wrote them. While we usually think of a prophet as someone who foretells the future, prophets in the Bible were given the task of speaking on God's behalf.

God sent the prophets to warn the nations, and in particular the nation of Israel, of the peril of their sinful choices. Some of the prophets used symbolic imagery to convey their messages and some did foretell of future events. Isaiah 53 describes the crucifixion of Jesus in considerable detail 700 years before the event happened.

The New Testament

The structure of the New Testament books is similar to the Old Testament. It also has three types of literature: history, letters and prophecy. There are five history books named Matthew, Mark, Luke, John and the Acts of the Apostles (usually just called the book of Acts).

The first four books are called the gospels and they are named for the person who wrote them. The gospels tell the history of Jesus and include His teachings and a record of the things He did. The first three gospels are very similar, telling many of the same stories about Jesus. Consequently, Bible scholars refer to them as the synoptic gospels, as they are quite synonymous. The gospel of John is rather different, telling many stories not included in the others. This is intentional as John's gospel was written quite a bit later than the others and he was intentionally providing information that was not already known.

The gospels are followed by the book of Acts which relates the history of the early church, how it got started and how it grew. We follow the adventures of some of the apostles who are mentioned in the gospels, especially the

8

apostle Peter. And in chapter nine we meet a man named Saul. You may know him better by the Greek version of his name – Paul. He becomes the chief character in the growth of the church into the world at large. Paul wrote many of the letters which make up the bulk of the New Testament.

The history books are followed by a series of letters written by the leaders of the church to various individuals and local churches. These books extend from the book of Romans to the book of Jude, twenty-one letters in all.

The first set of letters, from Romans to Philemon, was written by the Apostle Paul. They have the name of cities and were sent to the church in that city (like Romans for the church that met in Rome), or they are named for the person who was receiving the letter (like Titus).

After Paul's letters you'll find the book of Hebrews. We don't really know who wrote it, maybe Paul, maybe not. And the rest of the letters are named for the person who wrote the letter.

And finally, there is one book of prophecy in the New Testament, the book of Revelation. It is a little challenging to read as it is written with very symbolic imagery and speaks of the last days of the earth. Even though it is hard to understand, it is still well worth the read, as it is clear that in the end Jesus Christ conquers all the evils of this world. A new heaven and new earth await all those who follow Him.

4

What's your first step?

Your first step is obvious, but may not be easy to do – get a Bible. If you already own a Bible, then you're set, unless the one you own is hard to read.

The first English language Bible that was widely distributed was the King James Version of the Bible. It was translated from the original languages in 1611, the same time Shakespeare was writing. It can sound beautiful when it is read aloud, but can be hard to understand. If you have a King James Version of the Bible, I would encourage you to purchase a more modern translation.

My website www.bestbibletobuy.com is designed to give you all the information you need to make your best choice when buying a Bible. Let me briefly summarize the major points here, then when you have a chance go check the website for more details.

Translations

The Bible was originally written in three languages. The Old Testament was written in Hebrew, with a few chapters written in Aramaic, and the New Testament was written in Greek. It was first translated into English in the fourteenth century and there have been many, many translations into English since that time.

My website includes a list of the most popular English versions that you can buy today. Since they are all translated from the same original text, the differences are more a matter of taste and style than substance. Choose one that you find easy to read and understand.

If English is not your first language, look for a Bible in the language you speak fluently. The website www.biblegateway.com has a list of Bibles in languages other than English. At the time I am writing this they list fifty other languages, some with several options for translations. Click the down arrow to see the list of translations and scroll down to see all the language choices. They don't sell Bibles, but you will likely be able to buy one online from a distributor.

Devotional Bible, Study Bible or Just the Text

The other important decision to make when choosing a Bible is to decide between a devotional Bible, a study Bible or a Bible with just the text of the Bible. Anything in the Bible that is more than the text was added by the editors or the publishing company. At the website www.bestbibletobuy.com you can explore the options for devotional and study material in each translation.

Devotional Bibles include small inspirational articles drawn from the text you are reading. Many are designed to help make a personal application of the adjacent scriptures. Study Bibles include commentary about the text of the Bible and also provide information about who, what, where, when and why each book was written.

If you are new to reading the Bible I would recommend that you stick with a Bible that has just the text, no extras, for now. Look for one that has an opening summary at the beginning of each book. This was written by the editor or publisher, but in a text only Bible they are usually brief. Some study and devotional Bibles are filled with so much extra material that it is hard to tell which part is the Bible and which part is not. Let the Bible speak for itself when you first begin to read.

If you've had some experience with the Bible, then you probably already own the Bible you should read through the first time. If your current Bible has devotional or study material, read it as you have time but let your first read-through be focused on the text of the Bible. Most of the Bible is pretty easy to understand and much of it is incredibly inspirational on its own.

If your goal is more academic, a modern language translation with study notes is your best bet. Look for one that will give you study notes on the background of the culture within which the book was written. There are even some Bibles available with notes on archeology if that is your interest. The New International Version translation has the most variety for study notes. You can see a list of your options at the translations page of www.bestbibletobuy.com.

5

If you're a beginner

If you are new to Christianity or are seeking to find out about it, I'm so excited that this book can be a small part of your experience. You're setting out on a wonderful journey that may very well transform your life.

The Bible says of itself that "The Word of God is alive and active. Sharper than any double-edged sword, it penetrates even to dividing soul and spirit, joints and marrow; it judges the thoughts and attitudes of the heart" (Hebrews 4:12). Prepare to have a penetrating experience, one you won't regret.

The foundation of Christianity is the man Jesus of Nazareth. Christians believe that He is the Christ (or the Messiah), the Son of the living God (Matthew 16:16), the one who created all things (John 1:2). They believe that He died on the cross to pay the penalty for all our sins. And they believe that He came back to life three days later to demonstrate that He is Lord (Romans 4:24-25) and to offer eternal life to all who will believe (John 3:16). That is the kernel of the gospel.

So, if you are a new Christian or exploring Christianity for the first time, start by reading about Jesus. The first four books of the New Testament describe Jesus' life and ministry, and that is where you should start. The letters that follow these books provide insight into the implications of all that Jesus did and all that He taught. They give us practical tools for applying Jesus' teaching to our everyday life.

You could just start at Matthew and read through to the end of Revelation, but I would not recommend that approach. The first three gospel books are very similar, as mentioned earlier. It is much more interesting to read one of the gospels, then read some letters, read another gospel, some more letters, and so on. If you want to try that pattern, there is a reading schedule at the back of this book that will take you through the New Testament in eighty days.

What to look for in the Gospels

Most of Jesus' teaching is very clear and to the point. In fact the people who listened to Him were amazed at the power and authority of His teaching (Matthew 7:28-29). This first time through, focus on the things that you clearly understand. Think about how they apply to your life. Think about the things He did and how he interacted with others. Look for examples from His life that you can use to measure your own thoughts and actions.

There will be some things Jesus said and did that may not make sense to you. Let them alone for now. The Bible is for everyone at every level of scholarship and experience. You can study and study it and still find more to learn. As you continue to grow in your understanding, things that did not make sense when you first read them will start to become clear. For now, focus on the parts that make sense.

What to look for in the Letters

In the same way that the teachings of Jesus are to the point, the letters are also very insightful. All the letters were written to help the first Christians know how they should live in light of Jesus' teachings and in light of His death and resurrection. Most of what you will read is very applicable to our lives today. It is remarkable how some of the verses look like they could have been lifted from a current newspaper, blog post or online newsfeed.

Most of the letters were written by the Apostle Paul. Some of the things he writes are written within a particular cultural context, but most of what he says transcends his own culture. Keep in mind that he was living in a very patriarchal culture.

While some of his precepts seem outdated, in light of further study, they are actually shown to be ahead of their time. As with the teachings of Jesus, the letters in the New Testament have something for everyone. Some of the writing only makes sense after intense study. But most of the content in the letters is very clear and will give you plenty to think about. Some parts are absolutely thrilling. I'm so excited that you will be reading them.

Before you jump to the Bible reading schedules take some time to read the last chapter, *One Final Note*. It offers some additional suggestions that will be helpful. Or read through the next two chapters. You may find them insightful.

6

If you have some Bible experience

If you have some experience with church and the Bible, I would like to make a guess. You have probably spent quite a bit more time reading in the New Testament than the Old. Your Old Testament reading has probably focused on Psalms and some of the history books. I'm guessing you haven't spent much time reading the Prophets and probably not much of the Law from the history books. . . . Was I close?

Some parts of the Old Testament are definitely easier to read than others. But you are missing out on some important foundational understanding of the New Testament if you merely dabble in the Old Testament. The Bible is like a finely crafted symphony. Each part supports and contributes to the whole.

In Acts 20:27, the Apostle Paul declares that he has given the Ephesian church the whole counsel (or whole will) of God. In reading the whole Bible, you too will be availing yourself of the whole counsel of God. Every book has a part to play in your spiritual growth. I commend you for your decision to take this journey. You will not be sorry.

Given the fact that the Bible is a long book, comprised of many separate books, starting at the front and reading through to the back can be challenging. Many people get stuck in the history books that contain the laws for Israel that were given to Moses. The Ten Commandments, which you know about, are just the summary of many Jewish laws. It can be somewhat tiresome reading.

Other readers get through the history and poetry, then get stuck in the Prophecy books. Some of them are quite long, and they were written within a historical and cultural context that is quite distant from our own. Some use symbolic terms to describe their experiences. Without a reading schedule I usually got stuck in the Prophecy books. But once I had a reading schedule it was smooth sailing.

I recommend that, in light of the challenging parts of the Old Testament, you read the Old Testament and the New Testament concurrently. One of the reading schedules provided in the appendices of this book includes a schedule that provides daily portions of the Old Testament and New Testament to be read on the same day. The New Testament portion is about half the size of the Old Testament part. When the Old Testament reading is a bit dry or difficult, the New Testament provides a nice balance. Sticking to this schedule you can read through the Bible in a year, if you read every day

What to look for in the History books

The first five books of the Bible were written by Moses and are referred to as the Torah by Jewish and Christian Bible scholars. They establish the relationship that God has with mankind before Jesus came and describe how the nation of Israel began.

The history book you know the best is probably the first book, the book of Genesis. "In the beginning God created the heavens and the earth." Nearly everyone knows the first verse of the Bible. In fact you may know many of the events in the first 11 chapters. They include creation, Adam and Eve, the fall from grace and banishment from the Garden of Eden. We learn of Cain and Abel, Noah and the ark and the Tower of Babel.

From there you may be hazy about what is next. We meet a man named Abraham. It is absolutely essential that you know his story if you are going to understand parts of the New Testament. The Apostle Paul refers to him extensively in his letters. God binds Himself in a covenant (contractual) relationship to Abraham, hundreds of years before the nation of Israel received the law that defined their relationship to God.

As you are reading the book of Genesis, look for the human qualities of Abraham and his descendants. Try to put yourself in their shoes. Their struggles with faith and morality are all too prevalent in our own lives. The book ends with the remarkable story of Abraham's great grandson Joseph. It's a real page turner.

The next book is Exodus. You may have seen a movie, either a live action movie or an animated one that dramatizes this book about Moses leading the Children of Israel out of Egypt. The real story is a lot less of a soap opera but much more powerful. And it marks the beginning of the nation of Israel. The events that happen in this book are still celebrated today by Jews around the world at Passover. Jesus draws many parallels between His own death and the Passover event.

Also in the book of Exodus, God begins to reveal the law to Israel. The books of Leviticus, Numbers and Deuteronomy outline the bulk of these laws. Some of this reading can be dry, even boring. And some of the laws seem bizarre (Don't boil a baby goat in its mother's milk! – Uhh, okay). But it's important to read them. You will have a much more grounded appreciation of the grace that is described in the New Testament if you have gone to the trouble of reading the whole law. Don't cheat yourself out of this experience.

The book of Numbers contains some law, but it also has some stories that are great reading. Included with the law and the stories though, are lists of unfamiliar names and lots of numbers as the nation takes a census on its way to the Promised Land. Wade through the hard stuff and relish the stories.

The rest of the history books chronicle the establishment of the nation of Israel in the land that God had promised them. They go through many ups and downs becoming a nation until finally they become a kingdom.

David and his son Solomon are strong spiritual and military leaders, and the kingdom is firmly established. All of this is covered in the books Joshua, Judges, Ruth, 1 and 2 Samuel and into 1 Kings.

After Solomon's reign, the kingdom goes into decline, splinters into two separate nations, Israel and Judah. Both are conquered by other empires. Judah is taken into captivity, but maintains its identity and is eventually allowed to return to their homeland. That ends the history books. This material is covered in 1 and 2 Kings, 1 and 2 Chronicles, Ezra, Nehemiah and Esther.

As you read these books look for the similarities between this very ancient culture and our own. They are striking. The stories recorded are very easy to understand and draw lessons from. The actions of the good kings are inspiring. The actions of the bad kings are sometimes baffling, sometimes funny, sometimes tragic. Doesn't that sound just like the governing authorities where you live?

What to look for in the Poetry books

The poetry books begin with Job. This book provides many insights into human nature and into the nature of God. As Job tries to make sense of the crushing tragedies that come upon him, one on top of the other, we see a struggle that is all too familiar. As he dialogues with his friends, you may find parallels with your own thoughts and experiences.

Job is given a great privilege near the end of the book and we are allowed to listen to his direct conversation with God. Listen for the things that God says to him and watch for the things that God does not say. Does He ever answer Job's questions? Does He need to? You be the judge.

I expect that you have had a chance to read some of the Psalms, you may even be able to quote Psalm 23. Most of this poetry was written by David, before he became king and during his reign. It's interesting to note his different attitudes. One thing about David, he is very genuine. He loves God, but wants God to treat his enemies the same way we often do. And he's not afraid to repent when he's gone wrong.

The Psalms can be a very real source of inspiration and consolation. Many of them begin in despair and end in triumph, especially Psalm 22 which has many verses that correspond to Jesus' crucifixion. The later Psalms are written by other poets than David. I especially appreciate those written by Asaph.

David's son King Solomon wrote the remainder of the poetry books. You will enjoy his proverbs; they demonstrate the extra measure of wisdom that God granted to Solomon. Ecclesiastes shows the breadth of thought and experience that Solomon brought to his relationship with God. Solomon is discouraged by many of the things he sees in life, but he ends with a strong reliance on God.

The final book of poetry is surprising to find in a holy book. It is a love poem between a bride and groom. Try not to blush as you read it. Its inclusion is an endorsement of matrimonial passion. I find it encouraging to see that the Bible acknowledges all aspects of our lives.

What to look for in the Prophecy books

The Old Testament concludes with the Prophecy books. The history books record the facts about the ups and downs of Israel's relationship with God. One generation would be devoted and obedient and the next would be disobedient to the point of perversion.

In the prophecy books you will read this history from God's perspective. In speaking for God, the prophets allow us to experience His thoughts and feelings. These books show that God is not a distant deity watching unconcerned from afar. Unfaithfulness and ingratitude break His heart.

As you read through the prophecy books, let your heart and mind resonate with all the prophet is saying. Some of it may be hard to understand. Some of the prophets engage in unusual behavior at God's instruction to demonstrate a point that needs to be made clear. This is not unusual in a culture that had limited means of communication. Some of the prophets use symbolic language, but there are important lessons for us in these books.

Countries other than Israel and Judah are mentioned in some of the prophecy books but by names that you won't recognize. The names used in the Bible give it historic credibility as scholars can date the writing by these notations.

As with the other sections of the Bible, focus on what you understand. The message is unmistakable that God loves those He has created. But He dare not tolerate disobedience any more than a good parent would. After reading the history books you will be able to appreciate the prophecy books and the extent to which God must go to bring those He loves to repentance and restoration. And a thoughtful reading of the prophecy books will give you a much stronger appreciation of the grace that is offered through Jesus.

The New Testament

My guess is that you are probably comfortable with the contents of the New Testament. If a review would be helpful, go to the previous chapter and read through the sections that were written for those who have limited experience with the Bible.

If you're as familiar with the New Testament as I suspect, I encourage you to read through it this time with extra energy. Start making correlations between what you read in the New Testament and what you are reading in the Old Testament.

Are there things that Jesus says that draw from what you've been reading about Israel's history or from the poetry books? Has Jesus done or said something that was foreshadowed in a prophecy book? Is the Apostle Paul referring to a part of the law that makes more sense now that you've read the law in context?

It's amazing how the Old and New Testaments are finely integrated. The Bible is one book with a consistent message.

7

If you're on an academic quest

If you are reading the Bible for academic reasons, you are on a noble quest that many have taken before you. Your goal for this journey will have some bearing on how you want to approach this reading.

My recommendation is that you start at the beginning and read through to the end in the order in which the Bible books are listed. There is a reading schedule at the end of this book that provides 300 daily reading portions. If you read six days a week you'll be finished in 50 weeks.

The goal of this exercise may be facilitated by choosing a translation of the Bible that will give you additional information based on your particular interest. If the Bible appeals to you as a historical or cultural document, there are study Bibles that supply commentary of this nature. Check out some of these options online, at your local Christian book store or go to www.bestbibletobuy.com,

Many people have read the Bible as part of an academic exercise to compare the major world religions. If this is your goal, let me say that I admire your approach. May I make two suggestions? First, get a modern language copy of the Bible that has just the text of the Bible, no comments by the editors or the publisher. Let the Bible speak for itself.

Second, let the Bible be the last book you read in this endeavor. Others who have taken this journey have noted that the Bible is markedly different in nature from all other religious holy books. Saving it for last will give you the best possible position from which to make a comparison.

Whatever your motivation for reading the Bible, I believe I should give you fair warning. There are numerous accounts of people who start reading the Bible with the detachment of an academic. Somewhere along the journey, though, the detachment disappears and is replaced by conviction and belief.

As I said to those who are reading the Bible for the first time, the Bible says that it is "alive and active. Sharper than any double-edged sword, it penetrates even to dividing soul and spirit, joints and marrow; it judges the thoughts and attitudes of the heart" (Hebrews 4:12).

Keep your mind open to what you will be reading. Ask yourself what it means not only historically, culturally or comparatively, but what it means to you, especially as you read the New Testament.

If you have not read the two previous chapters they will give you a helpful overview of what you will be reading in each section of the Old and New Testaments.

8

One final note

I want to give you some final suggestions before you begin. I believe the Bible is God's Word, written by Him through the men He chose. It deserves your best effort and undivided attention.

As much as you are able, try to read the Bible at the same time every day. If you can fit a time for reading into a routine, that will help you be consistent. Try to tie it to some activity that you already do routinely, like eating lunch, a daily walk to the park or while you're waiting to pick up your kids.

Try to find a quiet place where you can be alone and undisturbed. I know this can be quite a challenge for busy moms and dads. If you need to get up a half hour early, it's well worth the sacrifice. Give yourself about a half hour for this endeavor if you can.

You may want to start with a short prayer. Ask God to help you see the truth of what you will be reading that day. Pray for wisdom to see how the passage might affect your life.

Be open to let God speak to you, but don't assume that every word you read is a special message just for you. Much of the Bible is a historical account of events. There may be lessons for you, but often the reading may not be special. Let God decide how and when He speaks to you. Just be faithful to respond when He does.

And if you're a Christian, and time and circumstances allow, it's great to have your quiet prayer time with God after reading His Word. This may not be practical if you're in a busy lunch room or on public transportation. But if you can, it can be rewarding to speak with Him about the concerns of your life directly upon reading the Bible.

Now, make your way to the Bible reading schedules and choose the one that fits your need. You're starting a journey that I hope will continue the rest of your life.

Bible Reading Schedules

This book includes three Bible reading schedules to help you read through the Bible in an organized and attainable manner. Choose one and read a portion as outlined each day. You may want to tuck this little book into your Bible so you can check off the daily passages as you read them.

Feel free to adapt these schedules to your time frame. Some of the schedules are quite ambitious, especially the last one. It's more important that you read the Bible in a thoughtful manner than it is to keep to a schedule. If you need to read a smaller portion on a given day, give yourself permission to do so.

These three schedules are available in a convenient single sheet format at my website

www.bestbibletobuy.com

They can be folded and used as a book mark. The first and third schedules were developed by me for programs at my church. The second schedule was given to me by my best friend. I don't honestly know who put it together, but it's the one I use regularly.

One word of warning: DO NOT let the reading schedule become a guilt trip. If you miss a day, you do not need to read two the next day. If you miss a week, simply start where you left off. It takes time to develop new habits. It's more important that you read the Bible with an open mind than it is to keep to a schedule, get discouraged and give up.

New Testament Reading Schedule

Each daily reading will take between 10 and 15 minutes. Read one portion each day and in less than three months you will have read through the New Testament.

☑ Book	Chapters	☑ Book	Chapters
☐ Luke	1-2	☐ Mark	8-9
☐	3-5	☐	10-11
☐	6-7	☐	12-13
☐	8-9	☐	14-16
☐	10-11	☐ 1 Corinthians	1-4
☐	12-14	☐	5-9
☐	15-17	☐	10-13
☐	18-20	☐	14-16
☐	21-22	☐ 2 Corinthians	1-5
☐	23-24	☐	6-9
☐ Acts	1-3	☐	10-13
☐	4-6	☐ 1 Timothy	1-6
☐	7-8	☐ 2 Timothy	1-4
☐	9-10	☐ Titus	1-3
☐	11-13	☐ Philemon	1
☐	14-16	☐ 2 John	1
☐	17-19	☐ 3 John	1
☐	20-22	☐ Jude	1
☐	23-26	☐ Matthew	1-4
☐	27-28	☐	5-7
☐ Galatians	1-3	☐	8-10
☐	4-6	☐	11-12
☐ Ephesians	1-3	☐	13-14
☐	4-6	☐	15-17
☐ Philippians	1-4	☐	18-20
☐ Colossians	1-4	☐	21-22
☐ Mark	1-3	☐	23-24
☐	4-5	☐	25-26
☐	6-7	☐	27-28

☑ Book	Chapters	☑ Book	Chapters
Romans	1-3	1 John	1-5
	4-7	1 Thessalonians	1-5
	8-11	2 Thessalonians	1-3
	12-16	1 Peter	1-5
Hebrews	1-5	2 Peter	1-3
	6-10	Revelation	1-4
	11-13		5-9
James	1-5		10-14
John	1-2		15-18
	3-4		19-22
	5-6		
	7-8		
	9-10		
	11-12		
	13-15		
	16-18		
	19-21		

Now that you've read through the New Testament, keep up the momentum. Try your hand at reading through the whole Bible using Appendix B.

Daily Bible Reading Schedule 1

This reading schedule will provide an orderly way to read through the Bible in a year if you read each day. But this will take discipline. It is designed to read a portion in the morning and evening. However, you find the best way and time to make this part of each day.

☑		Morning	☑		Evening
☐	Genesis	1-2	☐	Matthew	1
☐		3-5	☐		2
☐		6-8	☐		3
☐		9-11	☐		4
☐		12-14	☐		5:1-26
☐		15-17	☐		5:27-48
☐		18-19	☐		6
☐		20-22	☐		7
☐		23-24	☐		8
☐		25-26	☐		9:1-17
☐		27-28	☐		9:18-38
☐		29-30	☐		10:1-23
☐		31-32	☐		10:24-42
☐		33-35	☐		11
☐		36-37	☐		12:1-21
☐		38-40	☐		12:22-50
☐		41	☐		13:1-32
☐		42-43	☐		13:33-58
☐		44-45	☐		14:1-21
☐		46-48	☐		14:22-36
☐		49-50	☐		15:1-20
☐	Exodus	1-3	☐		15:21-39
☐		4-6	☐		16
☐		7-8	☐		17
☐		9-10	☐		18:1-20
☐		11-12	☐		18:21-35

☑	Morning		☑	Evening	
	Exodus	13-15		Matthew	19:1-15
		16-18			19:16-30
		19-21			20:1-16
		22-24			20:17-34
		25-26			21:1-22
		27-28			21:23-46
		29-30			22:1-22
		31-33			22:23-46
		34-36			23:1-22
		37-38			23:23-39
		39-40			24:1-22
	Leviticus	1-3			24:23-51
		4-6			25:1-30
		7-9			25:31-46
		10-12			26:1-19
		13			26:20-54
		14			26:55-75
		15-17			27:1-31
		18-19			27:32-66
		20-21			28:1-20
		22-23		Mark	1:1-22
		24-25			1:23-45
		26-27			2
	Numbers	1-2			3:1-21
		3-4			3:22-35
		5-6			4:1-20
		7			4:21-41
		8-10			5:1-20
		11-13			5:21-43
		14-15			6:1-32
		16-17			6:33-56
		18-20			7:1-13
		21-22			7:14-37
		23-25			8:1-21
		26-27			8:22-38
		28-29			9:1-29
		30-31			9:30-50
		32-33			10:1-31
		34-36			10:32-52
	Deuteronomy	1-2			11:1-19

	Morning			Evening
☐	Deuteronomy	3-4	☐	Mark	11:20-33
☐		5-7	☐		12:1-27
☐		8-10	☐		12:28-44
☐		11-13	☐		13:1-13
☐		14-16	☐		13:14-37
☐		17-19	☐		14:1-25
☐		20-22	☐		14:26-50
☐		23-25	☐		14:51-72
☐		26-27	☐		15:1-26
☐		28	☐		15:27-47
☐		29-30	☐		16
☐		31-32	☐	Luke	1:1-23
☐		33-34	☐		1:24-56
☐	Joshua	1-3	☐		1:57-80
☐		4-6	☐		2:1-24
☐		7-8	☐		2:25-52
☐		9-10	☐		3
☐		11-13	☐		4:1-32
☐		14-15	☐		4:33-44
☐		16-18	☐		5:1-16
☐		19-20	☐		5:17-39
☐		21-22	☐		6:1-26
☐		23-24	☐		6:27-49
☐	Judges	1-2	☐		7:1-30
☐		3-5	☐		7:31-50
☐		6-7	☐		8:1-21
☐		8-9	☐		8:22-56
☐		10-11	☐		9:1-36
☐		12-14	☐		9:37-62
☐		15-17	☐		10:1-24
☐		18-19	☐		10:25-42
☐		20-21	☐		11:1-28
☐	Ruth	1-4	☐		11:29-54
☐	1 Samuel	1-3	☐		12:1-34
☐		4-6	☐		12:35-59
☐		7-9	☐		13:1-21
☐		10-12	☐		13:22-35
☐		13-14	☐		14:1-24
☐		15-16	☐		14:25-35
☐		17-18	☐		15:1-10

☑	Morning		☑	Evening	
	1 Samuel	19-21		Luke	15:11-32
		22-24			16:1-18
		25-26			16:19-31
		27-29			17:1-19
		30-31			17:20-37
	2 Samuel	1-3			18:1-17
		4-6			18:18-43
		7-9			19:1-28
		10-12			19:29-48
		13-14			20:1-26
		15-16			20:27-47
		17-18			21:1-19
		19-20			21:20-38
		21-22			22:1-30
		23-24			22:31-53
	1 Kings	1-2			22:54-71
		3-5			23:1-26
		6-7			23:27-38
		8-9			23:39-56
		10-11			24:1-35
		12-13			24:36-53
		14-15		John	1:1-28
		16-18			1:29-51
		19-20			2
		21-22			3:1-21
	2 Kings	1-3			3:22-36
		4-5			4:1-30
		6-8			4:31-54
		9-11			5:1-24
		12-14			5:25-47
		15-17			6:1-21
		18-19			6:22-44
		20-22			6:45-71
		23-25			7:1-31
	1 Chronicles	1-2			7:32-53
		3-5			8:1-20
		6-7			8:21-36
		8-10			8:37-59
		11-13			9:1-23
		14-16			9:24-41

42

☑	Morning		☑	Evening	
	1 Chronicles	17-19		John	10:1-21
		20-22			10:22-42
		23-25			11:1-17
		26-27			11:18-46
		28-29			11:47-57
	2 Chronicles	1-3			12:1-19
		4-6			12:20-50
		7-9			13:1-17
		10-12			13:18-38
		13-16			14
		17-19			15
		20-22			16:1-15
		23-25			16:16-33
		26-28			17
		29-31			18:1-23
		32-33			18:24-40
		34-36			19:1-22
	Ezra	1-2			19:23-42
		3-5			20
		6-8			21
		9-10		Acts	1
	Nehemiah	1-3			2:1-13
		4-6			2:14-47
		7-8			3
		9-11			4:1-22
		12-13			4:23-32
	Esther	1-3			5:1-16
		4-6			5:17-42
		7-10			6
	Job	1-3			7:1-19
		4-6			7:20-43
		7-9			7:44-60
		10-12			8:1-25
		13-15			8:26-40
		16-18			9:1-22
		19-20			9:23-43
		21-22			10:1-23
		23-25			10:24-48
		26-28			11
		29-30			12

☑		Morning	☑		Evening
	Job	31-32		Acts	13:1-23
		33-34			13:24-52
		35-37			14
		38-39			15:1-21
		40-42			15:22-41
	Psalms	1-3			16:1-15
		4-6			16:16-40
		7-9			17:1-15
		10-12			17:16-34
		13-16			18
		17-18			19:1-20
		19-21			19:21-41
		22-24			20:1-16
		25-27			20:17-38
		28-30			21:1-14
		31-33			21:15-40
		34-35			22
		36-37			23:1-11
		38-40			23:12-35
		41-43			24
		44-46			25
		47-49			26
		50-52			27:1-25
		53-55			27:26-44
		56-58			28:1-15
		59-61			28:16-31
		62-64		Romans	1
		65-67			2
		68-69			3
		70-72			4
		73-74			5
		75-77			6
		78			7
		79-81			8:1-18
		82-84			8:19-39
		85-87			9
		88-89			10
		90-92			11:1-21
		93-95			11:22-36
		96-98			12

44

☑	Morning		☑	Evening	
	Psalms	99-102		Romans	13
		103-104			14
		105-106			15:1-20
		107-108			15:21-33
		109-111			16
		112-115		1 Corinthians	1
		116-118			2
		119:1-48			3
		119:49-104			4
		119:105-176			5
		120-123			6
		124-127			7:1-24
		128-131			7:25-40
		132-135			8
		136-138			9
		139-141			10:1-13
		142-144			10:14-33
		145-147			11:1-15
		148-150			11:16-34
	Proverbs	1-2			12
		3-4			13
		5-6			14:1-20
		7-8			14:21-40
		9-10			15:1-32
		11-12			15:33-58
		13-14			16
		15-16		2 Corinthians	1
		17-18		2 Cor	2
		19-20		2 Cor	3
		21-22		2 Cor	4
		23-24		2 Cor	5
		25-27		2 Cor	6
		28-29		2 Cor	7
		30-31		2 Cor	8
	Ecclesiastes	1-3		2 Cor	9
		4-6		2 Cor	10
		7-9		2 Cor	11:1-15
		10-12		2 Cor	11:16-33
	Song of Solomon	1-3		2 Cor	12
		4-5		2 Cor	13

45

☑	Morning		☑	Evening	
	Song of Solomon	6-8		Galatians	1
	Isaiah	1-3			2
		4-6			3
		7-9			4
		10-12			5
		13-15			6
		16-18		Ephesians	1
		19-21			2
		22-23			3
		24-26			4
		27-28			5
		29-30			6
		31-33		Philippians	1
		34-36			2
		37-38			3
		39-40			4
		41-42		Colossians	1
		43-44			2
		45-47			3
		48-49			4
		50-52		1 Thessalonians	1
		53-55			2
		56-58			3
		59-61			4
		62-64			5
		65-66		2 Thessalonians	1
	Jeremiah	1-2			2
		3-4			3
		5-6		1 Timothy	1
		7-8			2
		9-10			3
		11-13			4
		14-16			5
		17-19			6
		20-22		2 Timothy	1
		23-24			2
		25-26			3
		27-28			4
		29-30		Titus	1
		31-32			2

☑	Morning		☑	Evening	
	Jeremiah	33-35		Titus	3
		36-37		Philemon	1
		38-39		Hebrews	1
		40-42			2
		43-45			3
		46-48			4
		49-50			5
		51-52			6
	Lamentations	1-2			7
		3-5			8
	Ezekiel	1-3			9
		4-6			10:1-23
		7-9			10:24-39
		10-12			11:1-19
		13-15			11:20-40
		16			12
		17-19			13
		20-21		James	1
		22-23			2
		24-26			3
		27-28			4
		29-31			5
		32-33		1 Peter	1
		34-35			2
		36-37			3
		38-39			4
		40			5
		41-42		2 Peter	1
		43-44			2
		45-46			3
		47-48		1 John	1
	Daniel	1-2			2
		3-4			3
		5-6			4
		7-8			5
		9-10		2 John	1
		11-12		3 John	1
	Hosea	1-4		Jude	1
		5-8		Revelation	1
		9-11			2

☑	Morning		☑	Evening	
	Hosea	12-14		Revelation	3
	Joel	1-3			4
	Amos	1-3			5
		4-6			6
		7-9			7
	Obadiah	1			8
	Jonah	1-4			9
	Micah	1-3			10
		4-5			11
		6-7			12
	Nahum	1-3			13
	Habakkuk	1-3			14
	Zephaniah	1-3			15
	Haggai	1-2			16
	Zechariah	1-3			17
		4-6			18
		7-9			19
		10-12			20
		13-14			21
	Malachi	1-4			22

Daily Bible Reading Schedule 2

This reading schedule will take you through the Bible from start to finish in 50 weeks if you read six days a week.

	☑	Reading Portions		☑	Reading Portions
1		Genesis 1-2	27		Exodus 29-32
2		Genesis 3-4	28		Exodus 33-36
3		Genesis 5-6	29		Exodus 37-40
4		Genesis 7-9	30		Leviticus 1-5
5		Genesis 10-11	31		Leviticus 6-9
6		Genesis 12-14	32		Leviticus 10-13
7		Genesis 15-18	33		Leviticus 14-16
8		Genesis 19-21	34		Leviticus 17-20
9		Genesis 22-24	35		Leviticus 21-24
10		Genesis 25-27	36		Leviticus 25-27
11		Genesis 28-30	37		Numbers 1-3
12		Genesis 31-33	38		Numbers 4-6
13		Genesis 34-36	39		Numbers 7-8
14		Genesis 37-39	40		Numbers 9-12
15		Genesis 40-41	41		Numbers 13-15
16		Genesis 42-44	42		Numbers 16-19
17		Genesis 45-47	43		Numbers 20-22
18		Genesis 48-50	44		Numbers 23-25
19		Exodus 1-3	45		Numbers 26-27
20		Exodus 4-6	46		Numbers 28-30
21		Exodus 7-9	47		Numbers 31-32
22		Exodus 10-12	48		Numbers 33-36
23		Exodus 13-15	49		Deuteronomy 1-3
24		Exodus 16-19	50		Deuteronomy 4-6
25		Exodus 20-24	51		Deuteronomy 7-11
26		Exodus 25-28	52		Deuteronomy 12-16

53		Deuteronomy 17-21
54		Deuteronomy 22-26
55		Deuteronomy 27-29
56		Deuteronomy 30-34
57		Joshua 1-5
58		Joshua 6-9
59		Joshua 10-13
60		Joshua 14-17
61		Joshua 18-21
62		Joshua 22-24 &
		Judges 1
63		Judges 2-5
64		Judges 6-8
65		Judges 9-11
66		Judges 12-16
67		Judges 17-21
68		Ruth 1-4
69		1 Samuel 1-5
70		1 Samuel 6-10
71		1 Samuel 11-14
72		1 Samuel 15-17
73		1 Samuel 18-22
74		1 Samuel 23-27
75		1 Samuel 28-31 &
		2 Samuel 1-2
76		2 Samuel 3-8
77		2 Samuel 9-14
78		2 Samuel 15-19
79		2 Samuel 20-24
80		1 Kings 1-4
81		1 Kings 5-8
82		1 Kings 9-12
83		1 Kings 13-17
84		1 Kings 18-21
85		1 Kings 22 &
		2 Kings 1-4

86		2 Kings 5-9
87		2 Kings 10-14
88		2 Kings 15-18
89		2 Kings 19-23
90		2 Kings 24-25 &
		1 Chronicles 1-2
91		1 Chronicles 3-6:48
92		1 Chronicles 6:49-9:31
93		1 Chronicles 10-14
94		1 Chronicles 15-19
95		1 Chronicles 20-24
96		1 Chronicles 25-29
97		2 Chronicles 1-6
98		2 Chronicles 7-11
99		2 Chronicles 12-17
100		2 Chronicles 18-22
101		2 Chronicles 23-27
102		2 Chronicles 28-31
103		2 Chronicles 32-36
104		Ezra 1-5
105		Ezra 6-10
106		Nehemiah 1-6
107		Nehemiah 7-9
108		Nehemiah 10-13
109		Esther 1-6
110		Esther 7-10 & Job 1-2
111		Job 3-8
112		Job 9-14
113		Job 15-20
114		Job 21-27
115		Job 28-32
116		Job 33-37
117		Job 38-42
118		Psalms 1-8
119		Psalms 9-17
120		Psalms 18-22

121	Psalms 23-27	
122	Psalms 28-32	
123	Psalms 33-36	
124	Psalms 37-40	
125	Psalms 41-45	
126	Psalms 46-51	
127	Psalms 52-55	
128	Psalms 56-60	
129	Psalms 61-64	
130	Psalms 65-68	
131	Psalms 69-70	
132	Psalms 71-73	
133	Psalms 74-77	
134	Psalms 78-79	
135	Psalms 80-87	
136	Psalms 88-91	
137	Psalms 92-97	
138	Psalms 98-103	
139	Psalms 104-106	
140	Psalms 107-115	
141	Psalms 116-118 & 119:1-38	
142	Psalms 119:39-176 & 120-125	
143	Psalms 126-139	
144	Psalms 140-150	
145	Proverbs 1-4	
146	Proverbs 5-8	
147	Proverbs 9-12	
148	Proverbs 13-16	
149	Proverbs 17-20	
150	Proverbs 21-24	
151	Proverbs 25-28	
152	Proverbs 29-31	
153	Ecclesiastes 1-4	
154	Ecclesiastes 5-8	

155	Ecclesiastes 9-12	
156	Song of Solomon 1-8	
157	Isaiah 1-5	
158	Isaiah 6-10	
159	Isaiah 11-16	
160	Isaiah 17-22	
161	Isaiah 23-28	
162	Isaiah 29-33	
163	Isaiah 34-39	
164	Isaiah 40-43	
165	Isaiah 44-47	
166	Isaiah 48-53	
167	Isaiah 54-60	
168	Isaiah 61-66	
169	Jeremiah 1-4	
170	Jeremiah 5-7	
171	Jeremiah 8-11	
172	Jeremiah 12-16	
173	Jeremiah 17-20	
174	Jeremiah 21-24	
175	Jeremiah 25-27	
176	Jeremiah 28-30	
177	Jeremiah 31-32	
178	Jeremiah 33-36	
179	Jeremiah 37-40	
180	Jeremiah 41-45	
181	Jeremiah 46-49	
182	Jeremiah 50-51	
183	Jeremiah 52 & Lamentations 1-2	
184	Lamentations 3-5	
185	Ezekiel 1-6	
186	Ezekiel 7-11	
187	Ezekiel 12-15	
188	Ezekiel 16-17	
189	Ezekiel 18-20	

		Reading Portions				Reading Portions
190	☐	Ezekiel 21-23		217	☐	Matthew 18-20
191	☐	Ezekiel 24-27		218	☐	Matthew 21-22
192	☐	Ezekiel 28-31		219	☐	Matthew 23-24
193	☐	Ezekiel 32-34		220	☐	Matthew 25-26
194	☐	Ezekiel 35-37		221	☐	Matthew 27-28
195	☐	Ezekiel 38-40		222	☐	Mark 1-2
196	☐	Ezekiel 41-44		223	☐	Mark 3-4
197	☐	Ezekiel 45-48		224	☐	Mark 5-6
198	☐	Daniel 1-3		225	☐	Mark 7-8
199	☐	Daniel 4-6		226	☐	Mark 9-10
200	☐	Daniel 7-9		227	☐	Mark 11-13
201	☐	Daniel 10-12		228	☐	Mark 14
202	☐	Hosea 1-7		229	☐	Mark 15-16
203	☐	Hosea 8-14		230	☐	Luke 1
204	☐	Joel 1-3		231	☐	Luke 2-3
205	☐	Amos 1-9		232	☐	Luke 4-5
206	☐	Obadiah 1;		233	☐	Luke 6-7
		Jonah 1-4;		234	☐	Luke 8-9
		Micah 1-4		235	☐	Luke 10-11
207	☐	Micah 5-7;		236	☐	Luke 12-14
		Nahum 1-3		237	☐	Luke 15-17
208	☐	Habakkuk 1-3;		238	☐	Luke 18-20
		Zephaniah 1-3		239	☐	Luke 21-22
		Haggai 1-2		240	☐	Luke 23-24
209	☐	Zechariah 1-9		241	☐	John 1-3
210	☐	Zechariah 10-14;		242	☐	John 4-5
		Malachi 1-4		243	☐	John 6
211	☐	Matthew 1-4		244	☐	John 7-8
212	☐	Matthew 5-7		245	☐	John 9-10
213	☐	Matthew 8-10		246	☐	John 11-12
214	☐	Matthew 11-12		247	☐	John 13-15
215	☐	Matthew 13-14		248	☐	John 16-18
216	☐	Matthew 15-17		249	☐	John 19-21

☑		Reading Portions	☑		Reading Portions

250	☐	Acts 1-3	277	☐ 1 Thessalonians 1-5
251	☐	Acts 4-6	278	☐ 2 Thessalonians 1-3
252	☐	Acts 7-8	279	☐ 1 Timothy 1-3
253	☐	Acts 9-11	280	☐ 1 Timothy 4-6
254	☐	Acts 12-14	281	☐ 2 Timothy 1-4
255	☐	Acts 15-18	282	☐ Titus 1-3 &
256	☐	Acts 19-21		Philemon 1
257	☐	Acts 22-25	283	☐ Hebrews 1-4
258	☐	Acts 26-28	284	☐ Hebrews 5-7
259	☐	Romans 1-3	285	☐ Hebrews 8-10
260	☐	Romans 4-6	286	☐ Hebrews 11-13
261	☐	Romans 7-9	287	☐ James 1-5
262	☐	Romans 10-12	288	☐ 1 Peter 1-5
263	☐	Romans 13-16	289	☐ 2 Peter 1-3
264	☐	1Corinthians 1-4	290	☐ 1 John 1-3
265	☐	1 Corinthians 5-9	291	☐ 1 John 4-5
266	☐	1 Corinthians 10-13	292	☐ 2 John 1 &
267	☐	1 Corinthians 14-16		3 John 1 &
268	☐	2 Corinthians 1-5		Jude 1
269	☐	2 Corinthians 6-9	293	☐ Revelation 1-3
270	☐	2 Corinthians 10-13	294	☐ Revelation 4-7
271	☐	Galatians 1-3	295	☐ Revelation 8-11
272	☐	Galatians 4-6	296	☐ Revelation 12-14
273	☐	Ephesians 1-3	297	☐ Revelation 15-17
274	☐	Ephesians 4-6	298	☐ Revelation 18-20
275	☐	Philippians 1-4	299	☐ Revelation 21-22
276	☐	Colossians 1-4	300	

Scripture used in this book

Most of the scripture verses used in this book are quoted from the New International Version (NIV) of the Bible, but not all of them. I have put them here as they read in the NIV and in the order they appear in the Bible. You can easily look them up and check the context.

Genesis 1:1
In the beginning God created the heavens and the earth.

Psalm 23:1
The Lord is my shepherd, I lack nothing.

Matthew 7:28-29
When Jesus finished saying these things, the crowds were amazed at his teaching, because he taught as one who had authority and not as their teachers of the law.

Matthew 16:16
Simon Peter answered, "You are the Messiah, the Son of the living God."

John 1:2
He was with God in the beginning.

John 3:16
For God so loved the world that He gave His one and

only Son, that whoever believes in Him shall not perish but have eternal life.

Acts 20:27

For I have not hesitated to proclaim to you the whole will of God.

Romans 4:24-25

. . . but also for us, to whom God will credit righteousness – for us who believe in Him who raised Jesus from the dead. He was delivered over to death for our sins and was raised to life for our justification.

Hebrews 4:12

The Word of God is alive and active. Sharper than any double-edged sword, it penetrates even to dividing soul and spirit, joints and marrow; it judges the thoughts and attitudes of the heart.

.

www.ingramcontent.com/pod-product-compliance
Lightning Source LLC
Chambersburg PA
CBHW021223020426
42331CB00003B/446